# Hogueras

# Bonfires

## Bilingual Press/Editorial Bilingue



Address:
Bilingual Review/Press
Hispanic Research Center
Arizona State University
Tempe, Arizona 85287
(602) 965-3867

# Hogueras

# Bonfires

Marjorie Agosín

*Translated from the Spanish*
*by Naomi Lindstrom*

*Critical introduction*
*by Juan Villegas*

Bilingual Press/Editorial Bilingüe
TEMPE, ARIZONA

First bilingual English-Spanish edition. First Spanish edition © 1986 by Editorial Universitaria, Santiago, Chile



ISBN 0-927534-07-X

Library of Congress Catalog Card Number: 90-84003

PRINTED IN THE UNITED STATES OF AMERICA

*Cover design by Robin Ravary*

*Back cover photo by Estelle Disch*

**Acknowledgments**

This project is jointly supported by grants from the Arizona Commission on the Arts, a State agency, and the National Endowment for the Arts in Washington, D.C., a Federal agency.

# INDICE/CONTENTS

# *Introduction*
# Agosín: The Road to Transgression

*Juan Villegas*
*University of California, Irvine*

In Chilean poetry, it is readily apparent that women poets writing outside Chile are producing texts more attuned to so-called innovative currents, ideologically as well as poetically, than those living and writing inside the country. Among the latter, such authors as Heddy Navarro, Teresa Calderón, Alejandra Basualto, and Carmen Berenguer can be mentioned as revitalizing the "feminine" tradition. Their renewing efforts have been especially focused on creating a female "I" who enjoys freedom in her relations with men, satirizing a male "you," making a place in poetry for women's domestic lives, or expressing a strong political commitment. As far as they have come from the poetry of older women, these authors writing inside Chile are still somewhat reserved about erotic experience and the body and unconcerned with metapoetry. That is, there is no persistent awareness that one is making poetry, no distancing oneself self-consciously from art itself. Women authors writing abroad, though, are more in touch with feminist issues, less reserved in the expression of sexuality—including lesbian references and subject matter—and are evidently in tune with current tendencies in world poetry, although their political content is no more marked. Among these poets, especially worthy of attention are Myriam Díaz-Diocaretz, Bárbara Délano, Cecilia Vicuña, Leonora Vicuña, and Marjorie Agosín.

Marjorie Agosín presents an interesting case. On the one hand, she has been living outside Chile for years, she teaches and does research in Latin American literature, she has written about women poets and participated in meetings and discussions on feminism, and she lives in an environment where these present-day issues in poetry are much in the air. In her first book, *Conchalí* (1980), she satirizes "man's world" and academic life. This rebellious stance, owing much to Nicanor Parra, linked her to antipoetry. The "I"/protagonist appeared as a liberated woman, but the poetic codes had not broken free of poetry as the male presence defined it at that time. Given the shifts in Agosín's poetry observable in her subsequent books, *Brujas y algo más/Witches and Other Things* (1985) and *Women of Smoke/Mujeres de humo* (1988), *Hogueras/Bonfires* comes as a surprise on first reading. After an increasingly rebellious "I," with man appearing as the antagonist and language growing aggressive, these poems seem to represent the triumph of woman in love.

*Hogueras/Bonfires* is divided into two sections containing unequal numbers of poems and differing in their thematic register and the state of mind of the lyric speaker. The first part comprises nearly the entire book (forty-six poems); the second part has only seven poems.

Many of the poems of the first section, brief and luminous, capture snapshots of erotic pleasure. Most of the texts center on details of the intimate moment, magnified through poetic transformation: meetings between the "I" and "you" in different geographical settings (Cuenca, Quito, Buenos Aires) where the enjoyment of sensual pleasure and her own body absorb the speaker. These poems appear to stand apart from the main tendencies of women's writing in the eighties, except in the daringly intimate self-revelations of the "I" and the power of the poetic images. The aggressive, sarcastic speaker seems to have disappeared.

The poem "Patience" depicts the dimension of sensuality and pleasure through the senses as the ultimate goal of existence:

If patiently
you touch
my thighs
you'll find
the light of
leaves,
the dreams of
chloroform.

The poem "Winter in the Plaza de Mayo," naming a place with enormous political and human resonances in the contemporary history of Latin America, comes as a shock, for the speaker appears to be aware only of her own body and its sensations and heedless of the reverberations and political meanings evoked by the space around her:

> As if in a prism
> I study myself
> from the equinox
> of my skin
> to my hands
> over and over
> clasping together
> or throwing out
> corn to the pigeons
> who make no secret of their moves.

A first reading yields the voice of a woman in love, abandoning herself to the beloved and her untrammeled revelation of physical pleasure.

But when one takes a close look at certain aspects of this section it reveals another possible route of interpretation, one that brings the poems into an especially original current in modern women's poetry. The female "I" takes on the role of guide to the "you" in the erotic encounter. She is free to name areas of the body traditionally consigned to silence, and she is the one who directs the love scenes.

Man is also shifted retroactively out of the leading role in Western history via an ironic reworking of some of the mythic male figures of history, as in the case of Robin Hood and Rodrigo Díaz del Vivar, El Cid. Especially revealing is the comparison of the protagonist of the epic poem with the Rodrigo Díaz who emerges from the two poems dedicated to him: "Advice to Rodrigo I" and "Advice to Rodrigo II." To begin with, Don Rodrigo is sexualized; next, there is an insistent emphasis on women's presence and importance:

> Look out,
> Rodrigo Díaz,
> when that woman
> spreads her legs
> bearing gifts of
> rain and randomness
> and transparent masks.

Liberation is also affirmed by the awareness of forming part of a poetic tradition and putting it to good use. In this respect, one procedure stands out for its striking success: the use of intertextuality, especially with Chilean texts.

The selection of writings referred to gives clues to the tradition within which the author wants to be recognized and to the poetic antagonist: Chilean poetry and "sacred" Chilean poets. The texts that provide points of poetic reference are not by Chilean women; they are poems produced by men that can be read as symbols of traditional masculinity. Using them in this way, the woman poet "one-ups" them by subjecting them to ironic feminizing treatment.

The poem "Ritual of My Breasts," whose dedication to Pablo Neruda strengthens its echoes of that poet's "Ritual of My Legs," is an example of a famous poem now shifted toward the feminine: a male text reworked from the space of a woman's body.

> My breasts,
> in their likeness, hold
> two ceaseless suns,
> a slather of pink sand,
> and they parch bone dry when they feed the world,
> when they're on display, alone,
> for a little bit of bread and misery.

The way in which the collection celebrates the loving couple is inevitably reminiscent of Neruda's 1924 collection *Veinte poemas de amor y una canción desesperada (Twenty Love Poems and a Desperate Song*, 1969) in the recurrence of certain themes and the earthy evocation of love. In Neruda's case, though, woman is the instrument—the object, really—of the male speaker's existential or personal self-realization. The passage of the years also has freed up what was unmentionable in Neruda's time. The "I" of *Hogueras/Bonfires* is incomparably bolder than the speaker in Neruda's love poems.

Intertextuality with Enrique Lihn's *La pieza oscura* (*The Dark Room*, 1978), the 1963 collection whose impact on younger poets has been great, is evident and explicit in the titles and dedications of some of the poems. Once again, though, inversion occurs. This time around, it is not the boy cousin's voice speaking in the poems but the girl's, and she ends up inviting him "into the dark room." The poem "Inside the Dark Room," to pursue one possible reading, shows the complexity of this poetic interweaving. The poem is dedicated to Rodrigo ("For Rodrigo") just as the previous one—"Mountains"—bears the legend "For Raúl Zurita." The juxtaposition seems to turn Rodrigo into a real being. But in one of the poems in this same series, "Family Members in the Dark Room," this Rodrigo is again identified with "Rodrigo Díaz." This identification suggests, in this poem and others, a possible reading in which the use of intertextuality is even more significant. The boy and girl cousins, in Agosín's version, come to be man and woman, and the dark room is the space where they live together. The inversion of the relations between the characters of the poem then stands for social transformation:

> In the dark room, Rodrigo Díaz, far from these precocious moves, full of
> the certainty that always comes to the rejected partner, the one whose love is stronger,
> we say goodbye. Outside, the members of the family are waiting for us, ceremoniously:
> cousin Eulalia, Cassandra and the kids, Robin Hood, my
> husband's allergies. That is to say: the forebears
> of another
> even darker
> room.

The poem that fully pulls together this feminist inversion of codes and myths is "A Somewhat Different Account of Paradise," a poem that takes one from a free Eve to an Eve dominated by man. At first:

> Eve wasn't bad—
> a long tall blonde
> like a whiff of seabreeze
> fanning herself, cool and naked,
> on a rock in Paradise.

The poem ends:

> finally she married Adam
> and he changed her name
> and told her:
>
> now
> slave of my flesh
> servant of my bones
>
> your name is woman.

Tradition is thus utilized to transgress tradition.

The second section of the book lends a disquieting note. "Webs Spun Among the Fires"—the title of this section—brings a change of pace: The lines grow longer and the tone becomes slow and pained. Joy turns to melancholy and sadness. The taking of pleasure in love seems consigned to memory.

The extremely beautiful and melancholy final poem ends:

> We are like a field of poppies, a single row of tulips. Suns
> and moons seep through our eyes and our bodies
> settle in for love, and the body dreams to remember love.
>
> Alone, all alone, but less alone now, imagining ourselves on a miniature
> voyage from your mouth to mine.

Marjorie Agosín has come a long way from her first published poems. These new texts could well become classics of contemporary love poetry. The lyric voice is free of moral prejudices, of taboos against naming the female body; it speaks aloud of intimate places traditionally kept in silence; it summons the presence of the love poetry of the West, then reutilizes and ironically reworks man's poetic discourse of love. The poems, though, can potentially be read in a context of even greater significance: In place of the traditional couple of love poetry are man and woman in history and in the present.

A reading with this idea in mind of the poem "Winter on the Beaches," which bears the dedication "To Juan," suggests a further move along these lines. If "Juan" is taken as a casual way of addressing the Don Juan tradition, thus reversing his magnification into a myth (of male tradition) and restoring him to a man, the poem takes on a feminist meaning. It moves away from the story the speaker tells and becomes a new reading of Tisbea's seduction when Don Juan comes ashore on the beaches of Tarragona. The "I" and the "you" lose the status of an individual "I" and her lover to acquire the resonance of Man and Woman:

> You come, alarmed and naked
> with the mouths left queasy
> by the twists and turns of the rivers of the tides
> we are a rocky stretch
> unearthed by
> seaside scenes.
>
> The angry winter wind
> lashes at us.

*Translated by Naomi Lindstrom*

# I

## *Las bocas del amor*

---

## *Mouths of Love*

# Bonfires

My head
is a jellyfish.
A giant mass
of sunflowers set afire
when you
wash my
hair.

## Hogueras

Mi cabeza,
es una medusa.
Una hoguera
de girasoles
mientras me
lavas los
cabellos.

## Mouths of Love

Everything turns into
festival
when
you take my clothes off
and
I perfume
the
mouths
of
love.

## Las bocas del amor

Todo se vuelve
fiesta
cuando
me desnudas
y
yo perfumo
las
bocas
del
amor.

## Fires

Like a weave enmeshed
in smoke
fire
stirs
in its primal encounter,
in that country of
blond woods,
running for
their lives
amid the
flames.

Inert as suns,
sifting through
the hands,
we go on loving
and some drunk
is asking them to talk to him
of life.

Among the meshes,
fire, assured in its gala colors,
undresses us,
howls in our skin,
initiating us
into its ashes.

## Fuegos

Como una urdimbre
en humaredas,
el fuego
se agita en
su encuentro atávico,
en ese paisaje de
rubias maderas,
apresuradas
por salvarse
entre las
llamas.

Inertes como soles,
filtrándose entre
las manos,
no cesamos en el amor
y alguien ebrio
pide que le hablen
de la vida.

Entre las urdimbres,
el fuego, seguro, en su gala de colores
nos desviste,
aúlla en la piel,
para inaugurarnos
en sus cenizas.

## Desire

Desire,
a gentle,
hesitant
tickle,
a golden crust
asleep
untamable
snuggling
nestled
in the skin.

## Deseo

Deseo,
cosquilla
leve,
vacilante.
Costra dorada
durmiente
indomable
acurrucándose
por la
piel.

## Patience

If patiently
you touch my
thighs,
you'll find
the light of
leaves,
the dreams
of chloroform.

If you come down
into the moistened
shiver
of my
lips,
you'll find
God
winking
at you.

## Paciencia

Si con paciencia
me tocas los
muslos,
encontrarás
la luz de
las hojas,
los sueños
del cloroformo.

Si desciendes
al humedecido
escalofrío
de mis
labios,
encontrarás
a Dios
guiñándote
un
ojo.

## Chestnuts in the Air

On my palate
I found a
chestnut,
tasty, smelling good
like lucky signs.

It tickled
my lips
they couldn't keep from smiling when
sagely
I bit into it,
throwing it
a wink.

Nobody was watching us
only the high bright sky
and we
were golden tangles
throbbing in the bloodstream
of the savory morsel.

The chestnut and I were swinging
back and forth
in the mouth's warm inside,
in the to and fro of the palate
in the bonfires
of desire.

## Castañas en el aire

En mi paladar,
encontré una
castaña
gozosa, aromática,
como los buenos augurios.

Me hacía cosquillas
en los labios
que se curvaban cuando
sabiamente,
la mordía,
guiñándole
un ojito.

Nadie nos miraba
sólo el cielo colorido,
y nosotras,
éramos madejas doradas,
latiendo en las arterias
del delicioso mordisco.

La castaña y yo
nos columpiábamos
en la tibieza de la boca,
en el vaivén del paladar
en las fogatas
del deseo.

## Skirts

*(Quito)*

Underneath
my skirts
you found
a bunch of violets,
panties gold
as moss,
present at the
celebration
of the skin.

In your eyes,
or through them,
I learned to see
the river,
the water twisted off its courses
by the light
a cat asleep
among the rocks.

I studied you so much,
I started to examine
you with care
so through self-examination
I could
come to be
like things
that give off light.

## Las faldas

*(Quito)*

Debajo de mis faldas,
encontraste
un manojo de violetas,
calzones dorados
como los musgos,
asistiendo a la
celebración
de la piel.

En tus ojos
o desde ellos,
aprendí a ver
el río,
los senderos del agua dislocándose
por la luz,
un gato dormido
entre los roqueríos.

De tanto mirarte,
empecé con esmero
a contemplarte
para contemplarme
y parecerme
a las
cosas
que
alumbran.

## The River

*(Cuenca 1985)*

We could have
dreamed beside
the river's
voice,
the interstices of
the water dreaming out
in the skill
of the traveled
kiss,
or
simply
awakening
face up
in the sweep
of stones
and memories.

We could have
dreamed of holy
water, freshly drawn
from the river,
of skirts of water
and strings of seaweed.

We could have
been a
single river,
a single
arm
of water.

## El río

*(Cuenca 1985)*

Podríamos haber
soñado junto
a la voz
del río,
las aperturas del
agua soñándose en
la habilidad
del beso
viajado
o
simplemente,
amanecer
boca arriba
en el recorrido
de piedras
y memorias.

Podríamos haber
soñado con agua
santa, recién
traída del río
con faldas de agua
y algas.

Podríamos haber
sido un
solo río,
un solo
brazo
de agua.

## In Cuenca

I kiss
your eyelids
stretching taut
flowing slowly
as a river
in full speed
of summer.

I kiss the
shadowy thickness
of your lashes
and bring back
light to keep.

## En Cuenca

Arqueada te beso
los párpados,
con la lentitud
de un río,
en la rapidez
plena del verano.

Te beso la
sombría espesura
de tus pestañas
y guardo
claridades.

## Dreamsounds

The sounds of autumn
are yellow censers
folding back into
the knives of
childhood,
where outsider sounds
full of butterflies and leaves
were the dangerous orgies
of children unprotected from the cold.

The sounds of autumn are the
streets of my city,
or the smell at the scruff of your neck
rolling in triumph
across a fan of
leaves just like
all hair,
all sounds,
warm,
just barely warm, deep purple, dense,
of beds
in autumn.

## Sonidos-sueños

Los sonidos del otoño,
son sahumerios amarillos
retrocediendo en
las navajas de
la infancia,
donde los ruidos ajenos
llenos de mariposas y hojas
eran las orgías peligrosas
de niños desabrigados.

Los sonidos del
otoño, son las
calles de mi ciudad,
o el olor de tu nuca inclinada
rodando triunfante
sobre un abanico de
hojas parecidas
a todos los cabellos,
a todos los sonidos,
tibios, amarantas, espesos
de los lechos
en el
otoño.

## Applause

We used to keep saying
that no one else could
love as
we could,
be so perfect
in the nude,
or that our bodies
made their moves
to applause
in time with
memory
regenerating
in the damp
of eyelids.

Although we
knew, as well,
that we were just
like all the rest
just like
the
night just like
no one.

## Aplausos

Repetíamos
que nadie podría
quererse como
nosotros,
ser tan perfectos
en la desnudez,
o que nuestros cuerpos
se movían llenos
de aplausos
al compás
de la memoria
recreándose
con la humedad
de los párpados.

Aunque también
sabíamos
que éramos parecidos
a todos
iguales
a la
noche parecidos
a nadie.

## Robin Hood Among the Pillows

From out of sleep, as it seeps across the glow
of sleepers,
we appear in waves,
in the colors of a green field full of poppies,
our hair runs down the flowering roots
of a pale, precocious half-sleep,

eight children gathered round us are scenes from our
loves.
But my eyes, open, deep into the paradise of here and now,
await you, Robin Hood,
all dressed in green,
heavily covered from head to toe
and you manage to erase me from the
darkness
for in your ribs
I come awake
and in your tongue
I come round to myself.

## Robin Hood entre las almohadas

Desde el sueño, que se extiende en el resplandor
de los dormidos,
aparecemos ondeando,
en los colores de un verde prado de amapolas,
el cabello nos traspasa las raíces florecidas
de una precoz y pálida duermevela,

los ocho niños a nuestro alrededor, son las escenas de nuestros amores.
Pero mis ojos, abiertos, sumidos en el paraíso de los presentes,
te esperan a ti, Robin Hood,
todo vestido de verde,
todo vestido de envolturas espesas,
y consigues borrarme de las
tinieblas
porque en tus costillas
me despierto
y en tu lengua
me encuentro.

## Robin Hood

It wasn't so much Robin Hood,
with me it was his hat,
those green plumes
tickling me
shyly,
swiftly,
between the buttock
and the thigh.

## Robin Hood

Más que Robin Hood,
me gustaba su sombrero,
esas plumas verdes
que me hacían cosquillas
tímidamente,
velozmente,
entre la nalga
y el muslo.

## Caribe Hilton

The night, a swirl of city
like a palm-frond fantasy
is loose and liquid
colliding with the wraparound
green sea:
the water
the Caribbean
lit up, darkened
best side to the camera
lying there in wait.
In the distance the alligators hide,
blurry flowers and long rats tails hang from the sand.

Hungry
pushing their way through the waves
they lurk behind warped windowpanes, eying
the supple bounce
of big blond heads of hair
of flawless smiles
of legs dyed bronze on other people's sunshines
the sunshine of leached lands.

Salsa cha cha salsa
deafening eyeglasses
salsa,
white priests
eating up the golden oracles
of someone else's memory
they dance
with ice between their lips
slightly sunken in like whips.

A ways off
on the other coast
a couple plunges into

## Caribe Hilton

La noche, alada céntrica
como una fantasía
de palmeras
es ligera, acuosa
tropezando con la verde redondez marina
del agua,
del mar caribe
que encendido y oscuro
posando, fotogénico
yace,
aguarda.
A lo lejos se ocultan los lagartos,
flores borrosas y largas colas de ratas se descuelgan de las arenas.

Hambrientos
con un terco caminar entre las olas
acechan tras los cristales cóncavos aguardan
los elásticos movimientos
de melenas rubias
de dentaduras completas
de piernas teñidas por un sol ajeno:
sol de tierras mordidas.

Salsa chá chá salsa,
gafas ensordecedoras
salsa,
de sacerdotes blancos
consumiendo los oráculos dorados
de una memoria ajena
ellos bailan
con el hielo entre los labios
ligeramente hundidos como látigos.

A lo lejos,
en la otra costa

undulating loving
nibbling slowly
amid the slithery sounds of palms and palm fronds
never too kind to
the fortunes of the barefoot.
The couple stalks the sunken stars of the Caribe Hilton and a spectre
of Miss Monroe
like burning blasts of wind devouring one another on Caribbean sands
sands of washed-up cans
they gleam with glimpses of the future

and not even rum
can slake that thirst
of that
other voice.

dos se hunden
ondulados queriéndose
mordiéndose lentamente
entre el traicionero rumor de palmeras y palmas
que no favorecen
el azar de los descalzos.
Ellos asediando las estrellas hundidas del Caribe
Hilton y un espectro
de Miss Monroe,
ellos como ráfagas incendiadas comiéndose en las
arenas del Caribe
arenas de latas deshechas
ellos clarividentes brillan

y el ron aún no
apaga esa sed
de esa
otra
voz.

## Buenos Aires

In this city
hemmed in by the sea,
smelling of everyone,
may as well
go looking for you.

You're closer
to love
than hatred
or in with the madmen
crouched in
the fragility of plazas.

You stand on vacillating corners
that never
outgrow
the curbside encounter.

In this city,
no use trying to lose me.
You're easy to trace
down well-worn trails
luminescent with memories and nights.

On your shoulders,
my head,
threatening you,
loving you.

## Buenos Aires

En esta ciudad,
cercada por el mar,
con olores a todos,
nada se pierde
con buscarte.

Estás más
cerca del amor
que el odio,
o junto a los locos
agazapados en
la fragilidad de plazas.

Estás en las esquinas vacilantes,
que jamás abandonan
la costumbre
del encuentro.

En esta ciudad,
no sacas nada con perderte.
Es fácil saberte
por los antiguos desfiladeros recorridos
fosforescentes de memorias y noches.

Sobre tus hombros,
mi cabeza,
amenazándote,
queriéndote.

## Winter in the Plaza de Mayo

As if in a prism
I study myself
from the equinox
of my skin
to my hands
over and over
clasping together
or throwing out
corn to the pigeons
who make no secret of
their moves;
to feed the pigeons
to rest the fingertips
against your hair
that casts out nightmares.

You share
a common future with my
hands
on this day
when birds
are singing
in the
Plaza de Mayo.

## Invierno en la Plaza de Mayo

Como en un prisma
me contemplo,
entre el equinoccio
de mi piel
y mis manos
que repetidas e incesantes
se abrazan,
o reparten
maíz a las palomas,
que no ocultan
los gestos:
alimentar palomas
reposar las yemas
en tu cabello
desterrador de pesadillas.

Tú también sigues
el destino de mis
manos,
en este día
donde las aves
cantan
en la
Plaza
de Mayo.

## The Red Shoes

*for Marilyn*

She no longer
follows orders
the silence of her
flowering hair spreads free.

She rises shattered
with her red shoes, crimson,
pulp-red,
stretching and binding
the edges
of her legs
red shoes, surprising,
swiftly running down
the sidewalks, heading
in a rather strange direction for
those bandaged feet
but the red-stained shoes
lead her to the
smells, the illusions
behind closed doors, the racks,
the clauses.

She with her red shoes
runs, kneels, drinks like a naked woman,
hypnotized
because the red
shoes bring out
the look in her eyes,
her thighs,
the ankles of a rambling woman
or a sorceress,
and the red shoes
leave her breathless,

## Los zapatos rojos

*Para Marilyn*

Ya no cumple más
el mandato,
se desata el silencio
del florido cabello.

Se alza estallada
con sus zapatos rojos, carmesíes,
granadas,
que estiran y rebozan
las orillas
de sus piernas,
zapatos rojos, sorpresivos,
rápidos recorriendo
aceras, marcando el rumbo
de una dirección un tanto ajena a
esos pies vendados
pero los zapatos enrojecidos,
la conducen a los
olores, a las ilusiones
tras las puertas, los estantes,
las cláusulas.

Ella con sus zapatos rojos,
corre, se hinca, bebe como desnuda,
hipnotizada
porque los zapatos
rojos acentúan
su mirada,
las caderas,
los tobillos de divagadora,
o de hechicera,
y los zapatos rojos
la dejan sin aliento,
y su boca

and her mouth
is a reddish
sigh
a buckle
tossed out
to the
air.

es un suspiro
rojizo
una hebilla
lanzada
en el
aire.

## Lady Death Came . . .

Lady Death came
treading on my
heels. She liked
my red shoes.

She seemed to want
to savor me
all the better to
annihilate me
later in
between the
sheets
like
you.

## La muerte anduvo . . .

La muerte anduvo
pisándome los
talones, le gustaban
mis zapatos rojos.

Parece que quería
saborearme
para después
liquidarme
entre las
sábanas,
como
tú.

## The Red Dress and Death

Lady Death
came in my room
with her
evil purple
brooms.
Captivated,
she pulled on
the red
dress of
my loves.

She made faces at me
scratching her invisible
nose.
She broke into a dance
skeletal, incredulous,
skinny as can be.

For one longed-for instant,
I was jealous of her slenderness,
her poised and perfect bearing,
the absence of her nose colds.

Quick as thought
the death's head
jumped in between the sheets
she tried to greet you
but you were sound asleep
snoring
missed all the excitement.

Lady Death
took her leave of me
promised to be back

## El vestido rojo y la muerte

La muerte
entró a mi alcoba
con sus
escobas
malvas-moradas-malas.
Cautivada,
se vistió
con el rojizo
traje de
mis amores.

Me hizo muecas,
se rascó la invisible
nariz
comenzó a bailar
esquelética, incrédula,
flaquísima.

Por un anhelado instante,
envidié su delgadez
su postura segura y precisa,
la ausencia de sus resfriados.

Agil, de repente
la pelona,
saltó entre las sábanas,
quiso saludarte,
pero tú dormido
y apacible
roncabas sin
enterarte de nada.

La flaca se despidió
de mí,
prometió que volvería

not for you, not
for me,
only for the red dress
of my sorrows.

ni por ti ni
por mí,
sólo por el vestido rojizo
de mis dolores.

## Mountains

*for Raúl Zurita*

She washed his face
she sought the familiar look
in his eyes,
she stroked his hair, a loosened mass of
smoke and stubborn tanglewood,
she cleaned out, horrified, the
open wounds
like names left
face down
in a riverbed.

She went back, distant
in the litany
of leave-taking,
alone, all alone,
to a house lost
out among
the mountain lands
of
Chile.

## Cordilleras

*Para Raúl Zurita*

Ella le lavó la cara,
buscó la familiaridad
de sus ojos,
acarició el desprendido cabello de
humos y reacios matorrales,
limpió asustada las
heridas abiertas
como los nombres
boca abajo tras
los cauces
de un río.

Ella, regresó lejana
en la letanía
del Adiós
sola, solísima
a una casa perdida
entre
las cordilleras
de
Chile.

## Inside the Dark Room

*for Rodrigo*

We came to cries and screams
and drawn and quartered
we became the light
that filled the room,
come together in the intermittent touch
of a kiss
that scurries off
only to reveal itself as
word.

Dizzy, passed from hand to hand,
you washed me clean, loving me
birthing me clean from miracles
clear through to the transparency
of the source that
swells and sways
within the mouth.

Your mouth, ever so slowly
pronouncing me with the tongues
of love,
that mouth exploding in the orifices,
opening in triumph to awaken
in the dark room,
dark, dark light yes full of light.

## La pieza oscura para dentro

*Para Rodrigo*

Entramos en los alaridos,
y descuartizados
nos transfigurábamos en la
luz del cuarto,
reuniéndonos en la intermitencia
de un beso
que huye para
saberse palabra.

Vertiginosos, manoseados,
tú me lavabas, amándome
naciéndome desde los milagros
hasta la transparencia
del origen que se
dilata y mece
en la boca.

Tu boca, lentísima que me
pronuncia, con las lenguas
del amor,
esa boca que se estrella en los orificios,
que se abre victoriosa para despertar
en la pieza oscura,
oscura, oscura, clara sí muy clara.

## The Dark Room

*to Enrique Lihn and Rodrigo*

Eager, wicked,
we came into the dark room
gravitating equally
to filth
to light.

We were setting out, in the
interstices of the air,
to put the world to rights.

Unhurriedly,
skirts came falling down
panties
They came falling down,
possessed and lithe,
into the dark astuteness
of your hands.

In the dark room, we eyed each other awkwardly
laughing with voices like paper knives.
Later we learned where to kiss, to lick, to wound.
Later we mastered the sweat of our breath.

In the dark room,
it was all too easy
to abuse each other in our love, like silence
moaning sounds.

We became the repetition
of bright clear woods
that trapped us in the whorls
of its skin.

## La pieza oscura

*A Enrique Lihn y a Rodrigo*

Entusiasmados, malévolos,
entrábamos a la pieza oscura,
como dos niños
gravitando entre la inmundicia
y la luz.

Ibamos en las rendijas
del aire
a resolverlo todo.

Calmadamente,
caían las faldas,
los calzones,
ajenos al pecado.
Caían enloquecidos y ágiles
en la oscura astucia
de tus manos.

En la pieza oscura torpemente nos mirábamos
riéndonos con voces de cortaplumas.
Después aprendimos dónde besar, lamer, herir.
Después aprendimos a contrólar el sudor del aliento.

En la pieza oscura,
si era posible desafortunadamente
maltratarnos, queriéndonos, como en el silencio
que gime ruidos.

Eramos la repetición
de un bosque clarísimo
que nos atrapaba
en las maniobras
de la piel.

Come along with me,
come join me in
the dark room.

Ven conmigo,
te invito a la
pieza oscura.

## Family Members in the Dark Room

We used to play without the cousins in the dark room. Remember
that,
Rodrigo?
and so we'd come together in the undergrowth of pillows
and snuggle down perversely, sweaty in the reddish jungle of the
bedclothes.
Burrowing beneath, we became a tunnel like a stretch of beach,
we were brave among
the dunes. Don't forget, Rodrigo.

In the dark room, we stroked nostalgia, as in
unseen silent movies. You would summon up, all flushed and
ruddy, the first
sleeping pubis, the first girl's voice, or those breasts,
swerving out like little pockets of cool water. We carried on
our secret meetings on the stained brocaded sofa, while
you and I glimpsed our reddened outlaw faces in the weirdness
of mixed-up adolescents, or in disappearing mirrors.

Now you and I in this dark room, yellowing and ghastly,
innocently take up love where we left off, maybe just from fear
of breaking habits.
We dream of being a delirious underwater crystal.
Desire with no past comes after us like mountain passes full of
blood and fire.

In the dark room, Rodrigo Díaz, far from these precocious moves,
full of
the certainty that always comes to the rejected partner, the
one whose love is stronger,
we say goodbye. Outside, the members of the family are waiting
for us ceremoniously:

## Familiares en la pieza oscura

Jugábamos sin los primos a la pieza oscura. ¿Lo recuerdas
Rodrigo?
y así, nos encontrábamos entre los matorrales de almohadas
para descender perversos, sudando en la frondosidad rojiza de
las sábanas.
Debajo de ellas, éramos un túnel parecido a una escena de la
playa, éramos valientes entre las dunas de la piel. No lo
olvides Rodrigo.

En la pieza oscura, aceitábamos nostalgias, como en las mudas
películas nunca vistas. Tú rojito, rosado evocabas el primer
pubis durmiente, la primera voz de niña, o esos senos largamente
arqueados como pequeñas bolsas de agua fresca. Repetíamos los
encuentros clandestinos en el manchado sofá de brocato,
mientras
tú y yo viéndonos ruborizados, traviesos en la anomalía de
extraños adolescentes o en los espejos esfumados.

Ahora, tú y yo en esta pieza oscura, amarilla y enferma.
Inocentes
nos queremos igual, aunque sea por el temor a quebrajar
costumbres.
Soñamos a ser un cristal delirando entre las aguas. El deseo,
sin historias nos persigue como desfiladeros llenos de sangre y
fuego.

En la pieza oscura, Rodrigo Díaz, lejos de la precocidad, con
la certeza que siempre habrá el abandonado, o el que quiere más
nos despedimos. Afuera nos aguardan ceremoniosos, los
familiares:

cousin Eulalia, Cassandra and the kids, Robin Hood, my
husband's allergies. That is to say: the forebears of another
even darker
room.

la prima Eulalia, Casandra, los hijos, Robin Hood, las alergias de mi marido. En fin, los ancestros de otra pieza aún más oscura.

## Families

We burn in the memory
of those who have been,
the terror of uncertainties,
the love of gentle bonfires.

We burn in a single wound
or in the split body
joining together to
disperse into
a single face
covering
the face
that's there to kiss.

Stretching out,
whose legs are
those
that we don't recognize,
being the arpeggio
of a tree,
of a thousand roots
caressing
every length
of a
single body?

## Familias

Ardemos en la memoria
de todos los que han sido,
terror de salvajes incertidumbres,
amor de benignas hogueras.

Ardemos en una misma herida
o en el cuerpo dividido
que se une para
dislocarse en
un solo rostro
cubriendo
el rostro
que se besa.

Extendidos,
¿De quién son esas
piernas?
que no las reconocemos
al ser arpegio
de un árbol,
de mil raíces
acariciando
cada longitud
de un
mismo cuerpo?

## Resemblances

Naked, we
resemble
neither death
nor desire.
We are, instead, two
rivers, two fish behind
the shadow,
two lizards
clenched
by a sun lulled drowsy
in the mist.

Naked we resemble
animals
at rest.
Or children's writing
seeking only sleep,
to be a body in the mists
or in the silence
of a common blood.

## Semejanzas

Desnudos, ya no nos
parecemos
ni a la muerte
ni al deseo.
Somos más bien, dos
ríos, dos peces detrás
de la sombra,
dos lagartijas
encrispadas
por un sol adormecido
en la niebla.

Desnudos nos parecemos
a los animales
en reposo.
O a la escritura de los niños,
que no pretende más que el sueño,
más que ser cuerpo en las nieblas
o en el silencio
de una misma sangre.

## Advice to Rodrigo I

Don't you forget, Rodrigo Díaz,
that woman's body
in the lost scenario
of her nakedness,
in the way her face contorts
when you
touch her.

Rodrigo Díaz,
don't you ever forget
the dangerous whimpers
flaring up
when you call her name
and she, amassed
of bleached-out deserts
moans
not following your lead.

She's the cautious siren,
nibbling at you, drawing you away
from the perfect features of that pseudoparadise,
and with that slithery swaying
she makes you see,
reveling in her danger.

## Consejos para Rodrigo I

No olvides, Rodrigo Díaz,
a ese cuerpo de mujer
en el escenario perdido
de su desnudez,
en sus muecas,
mientras tú la
tocas.

Rodrigo Díaz,
no olvides
los peligrosos quejidos
que se encandilan
cuando tú la llamas
y ella, plasmada
de desiertos blancos,
gime
sin obedecerte.

Ella es la sirena cauta,
mordiéndote, arrancándote,
de las perfecciones de aquel paraíso falso,
y entre esas pérfidas ondulaciones,
ella te enseña
gozosa de su peligro.

## Advice to Rodrigo II

Look out,
Rodrigo Díaz,
when that woman
spreads her legs
bearing gifts of
rain and randomness
and transparent masks.

Look out,
Rodrigo Díaz,
when she spreads
her legs
and you see her vivid
swarms
the honey of her
private places.

Don't forget one thing:
she's a staunch cathedral
for the celebration
of true
rites.

## Consejos para Rodrigo II

Cuidado,
Rodrigo Díaz,
cuando esa mujer
abre sus piernas
y te obsequia
lluvias, azares,
máscaras transparentes.

Cuidado,
Rodrigo Díaz,
cuando te abre
sus piernas
y ves sus enjambres
coloridos,
la miel de sus pudores.

No lo olvides,
ella es una catedral
segura
donde se ofician
las verdaderas
ceremonias.

## Celebration of Knives

So unafraid,
out of the depths
we stalked each other in this tiger summer
in the hidden eucalyptus, resting, restless,
under beds and bonfires.

We light the lights of air
the fireflies of the inconclusive moment
tempestuous and wicked
as you and I
stealthy delinquents of desire
they followed us,
bloodied
in the work of
love.

We see each other, gazing
down the darkness of the mouth,
or in the sweat of clear light bellies
smelling one another's odors, we plunge down into
the place where fire begins.

The wine hums a tune
undressing us among the ashen pillows
that darken us and hide us,
mingle us,
cradling us like waves.

So unafraid, I begin to strip
your sleeping veins,
full of sleepwalked dreams of me
I extract your jaws,
your dense eyes

## Celebración de las navajas

Tan sin miedo, y
desde el fondo
nos acechamos en este verano de tigres
y eucaliptus ocultos, reposando, inquietos,
debajo de camas y hogueras.

Encendemos las luces del aire,
las luciérnagas del segundo inconcluso,
intempestuoso y malévolo
como tú y yo,
fugaces delincuentes del deseo,
nos acompañan
ensangrentadas
en las faenas del
amor.

Nos vemos, mirándonos
en la oscuridad de la boca,
o en el sudor de los vientres claros,
olfateándonos, descendemos hasta el
comienzo del fuego.

El vino, canturrea,
desvistiéndonos entre las almohadas cenicientas
que nos oscurecen y encienden,
que nos confunden,
meciéndonos como las olas.

Tan sin miedo, comienzo a desvestir
tus venas dormidas,
que me sueñan sonámbulas,
extraigo tus mandíbulas,
tus ojos espesos

and they roll into
the firewood.
(Rodrigo Díaz, don't forget the chimneys.)

At the core of being
fire watches over us
and your
hands,
intrepid,
serious, respectful,
conceal that
knife
forever hidden
in the edge
of fire
like a major wound.

My head
spilled open,
dreams,
desires.

y ellos, ruedan entre
los leños,
(no olvides Rodrigo Díaz las chimeneas).

En el centro del alma,
el fuego nos vigila
y tus manos,
intrépidas,
serias, respetuosas,
esconden a esa
navaja
oculta desde
siempre en
el filo
del fuego
como una extensa herida.

Mi cabeza derramada,
sueña con los
deseos.

## Don Juan

Forgive me
for telling it
plain.
Don Juan
was a
lecherous,
half blind,
splay-legged
old man,
starting to go bald,
an overheated
peacock
with a weak
libido
out chasing after
the poor
village women,
sad victims
of the impotence
of Mr. D. Juan III, Esquire.

Isn't that right, Elvira?

## Don Juan

Discúlpame
por ciertas
verdades.
Don Juan Tenorio
era un anciano
libidinoso,
semi-ciego,
despaturrado,
y algo calvito,
un calenturiento
vanidoso
de libido débil
buscando a las
pobres mujeres
de aldeas,
tristes víctimas
de la impotencia
de Mr. Tenorio.

¿No es verdad, Elvira?

## Epitaph for a Coward

He loved her by surprise,
and in a hurry,
undid the perfect orifice
of his pants,
and coolly went back home
to sleep beside
his wife,
to dream about
the one he
loved
by surprise
in the tortured delirium
of his truth.

## Epitafio para un cobarde

La amaba sorpresivamente,
apresuradamente,
se desabrochaba el orificio perfecto
del pantalón,
y regresaba tranquilo a casa
a dormir con
su mujer,
a soñar
con esa que
amaba
apresuradamente
en los delirios
atormentados
de su verdad.

## Ritual of My Breasts

*to Pablo Neruda*

Today, I stand
before the tenuous
roundness of my breasts.
Two variations on
the little things,
they retain a smell
of things kept shut away,
of tortured moons
that reel and flare
when You
enfold them
tenderly
in your arms
or kiss them over and again
like two goblets or two domes
of water.

My breasts,
in their likeness, hold
two ceaseless suns,
a slather of pink sand
and they parch bone-dry when they feed the world,
when they're on display, alone,
for a little bit of bread and misery.

I love them, they come with me
without my giving them a thought
I contemplate them in their imperfections
as they're budding in or falling earth-
ward like the chestnuts
of my desires.

My breasts,
come loose,

## Ritual de mis senos

*A Pablo Neruda*

Hoy, aparezco
ante la redondez
tenue de mis senos.
Son dos variaciones
en pequeñeces,
guardan un olor
a encierro,
a lunas atormentadas,
que revolotean y encandilan
cuando Tú,
tiernamente los
guardas en
tus brazos
o los besas una y otra vez
como dos copas o cúpulas
de agua.

Mis senos,
guardan en su similitud,
dos soles incesantes,
un conjunto de arenas rosadas,
y se agrietan al alimentar al mundo,
al exhibirse solitarios
por un poco de pan y de miseria.

Yo los quiero, me acompañan
aunque pasan para mí desapercibidos,
los contemplo en sus imperfecciones,
mientras germinan o caen a la
tierra como las castañas de mis deseos.

Mis senos,
desprendidos,

modeling their curves
in skin,
are the mirrors
of your lips.

contorneándose en la
piel
son los espejos
de tus labios.

## Triptych

1.

I got his coffee
fried him up a
couple eggs.
He read
his paper
and we
said goodbye
forever.

2.

And now that
you abandoned me
Coca-Cola
went up,
what am I supposed to do
to put the sparkle
back in life?

3.

Let's see, let's see
if he's the cock of
all the walk
let everybody see.

## Tríptico

1\.

Le preparé su café,
le hice un
par de huevos fritos.
El leyó
su periódico
y nos
despedimos
para siempre.

2\.

Y ahora que
me abandonaste
que subió
la Coca-Cola,
¿qué hacer
para darle
chispa
a mi vida?

3\.

A ver, a ver,
el más gallito
que la
muestre
no más.

## Colgate

*to John*

Some day, we'll end up
breaking up
and all on account of
that damned
tube of toothpaste
that I squirt out
wildly here and yon
in the dark
sea of
the tiles.

And you patiently
press upwards, brush, and put away
as if it were
a spangle
lost
in the latest
earthquake.

Although perhaps, it just might be
easier for us
to have
two tooth-
brushes,
two Colgates.

## Colgate

*A John*

Algún día, acabaremos
por separarnos
y todo esto
por esa maldita
pasta de dientes
que yo desparramo
por azar,
entre el mar
oscuro de
los azulejos.

Y tú, pacientemente,
presionas, cepillas, guardas,
como si se tratara de
una lentejuela
extraviada
en el último
terremoto.

Aunque tal vez, sería más
fácil que tú y yo
tuviéramos
dos cepillos
de dientes,
dos Colgates.

## Wardrobes

He insists on
dressing me.
He starts out with the
sacrilege
of my dizzying
hose,
he transcends the pluralities
of passing legs
and I
allow
him to invent me
amid the mediocrity
of clothing
while strange
red blips
course by, piled high
as bonfires
this crackling
air
these garments
trapped
in the fiery glow
of my body
with no language.

## Armarios

El insiste en
vestirme.
Comienza por el
sacrilegio
de mis medias
vertiginosas,
trasciende las pluralidades
de piernas pasajeras
y yo
dejo
que me invente
en la mediocridad
de los atuendos
mientras extrañas
manchas rojizas
cruzan alzadas
como hogueras
este aire que
crepita
esta ropa
atrapada
en los resplandores
de mi cuerpo
sin idiomas.

## Eve

As you dream
or sleep
I fill you full
of fish,
of blue apples,
I ring you round with tiny lights
and five-leafed clover.

I become
a golden
serpent
I bite into you
over and over
remorselessly.

## Eva

Mientras sueñas
o duermes
yo te lleno
de peces,
de manzanas azules,
te rodeo de finas lucecitas
y tréboles de cinco hojas.

Me convierto
en serpiente
dorada,
te muerdo mucho
sin arrepentirme.

## A Somewhat Different Account of Paradise

Adam was sick of the same old scene
same cigarette stuck in his mouth
and sent out for some
Eve or Mary.
God was quick to correct the oversight
and sent a waking dream
or maybe he was dreaming in his sleep
he pulled out a rib, gleaming
like a mirror,
beat it like an omelette,
round and crispy, lots of onion:
and presto change-o
there was Eve
right by his side.

Eve wasn't bad—
a long tall blonde
like a whiff of seabreeze
fanning herself, cool and naked,
on a rock in Paradise.

Adam kept asking for this and that
something to drink
a little favor in between the legs.
Eve was on her knees, washing out his clothes
in the Euphrates
she brought him herbs
alchemy and seaweed
for Adam's bobbling throat.

Eve got pretty sick of Adam
telling her
come here
wash my hair
strike the flints and scramble up some eggs

## Nueva versión del paraíso

Adán se cansó del escenario vacío
del cigarrillo en la boca
y pidió que le trajesen a la
Eva o a la María,
Dios sometido y cabizbajo
lo hizo soñar despierto
o soñó dormido
le sacó una costilla dorada
como espejo
la amasó como tortilla española
redonda, fina, cebollenta,
y colorín colorado
apareció Eva
a su lado.

La Eva tenía buena pinta
rubia, flaca
con olor de aguas,
se abanicaba lejana, desnuda
en una roca del paraíso.

Adán le pedía cosas,
brebajes,
favores de intercambio y entrepiernas
Eva hincada lavábale la ropa
en el Eufrates
le traía hierbas buenas
alquimias y algas
para la movediza garganta del Adán.

Eva cansada del Adán
que le decía
ven pa cá
límpiame el cabello
frota las piedras para huevos revueltos

so
she went in on it with the serpent,
eating an apple
made like buttocks out of holy water.
Adam sank his teeth in, too
and that moment's pleasure
stuck forever
in his craw.

God wrote a big fat book
all about Adam's apple
only it was really Eve's
but Adam got to be the hero
and Eve was just a vessel,
then God got mad
accusing Eve
of disobedience
of snaky hips
he called her a plain and outright baldfaced sinner woman
they blamed all Adam's troubles on her:
his cold
the dry spell,
hurricanes, menstruation,
warps in mirrors.

Eve kept her mouth shut and
tied back her hair.
She meekly obeyed
Adam's son and Adam's apple
she took to prayer
and started getting fat.
She was as fat as the book God kept on writing.

She didn't sleep skinny.
She bought a Paradise Cotton nightie
from the catalogues of gypsy crones
wandering through one hundred years of solitude.

entonces
ella decidió aliarse con la culebra
comiendo una manzanita
con forma de nalgas y agua bendita
Adán también un mordisco le plantó
y la huella de esa delicia
en la garganta para siempre se
le quedó.

Dios escribió un libro gordísimo
para testimoniar de la manzana de Adán
que realmente era de Eva,
pero Adán protagonizó el cuento
y la Eva un mero instrumento
entonces Dios se enfadó
acusó a Eva
de desobediencia
de moverse como serpiente
de activa pecadora transgresora
la culparon de los males de Adán
de su resfriado,
de las sequías,
huracanes,
el flujo menstrual
y los espejos cóncavos.

Eva enmudeció
se amarró el cabello
sumisa obedeció
a los hijos de Adán y su manzana,
empezó a rezar
a engordar,
era tan gorda como el libro que Dios seguía escribiendo.

No dormía desnuda
compró un camisón de algodón paraíso
en los catálogos de las viejas gitanas

Eve was immaculate
the way God says to be
she conceived Adam's offspring
just like that.
They'd go on a picnic to the graveyard—
bam—one kid right after another
like trees spring up in the virgin forest.

Eve stopped drinking Gin & Gin
down by the Euphrates
she began to write a cookbook for the perfect fire
but never tried to one-up God
finally she married Adam
and he changed her name
and told her:
now
slave of my flesh
servant of my bones

your name is woman.

que viajaban por los cien años de soledad.
Eva fue inmaculada,
como Dios manda,
concibió los hijos de Adán
así no más,
iban de picnic al santo sepulcro
y boom nacían los chiquillos
como arbustos silvestres en una selva virgen.

Eva dejó de beber Gin con Gin
en la orilla del Eufrates
comenzó a escribir un libro de recetas para el fuego perfecto
aunque nunca le hizo la competencia a Dios
finalmente se casó con Adán
él le cambió de nombre
y le dijo
ahora
esclava de mi carne
sirvienta de mis huesos

te llamarás mujer.

## Marilyn Monroe

Marilyn Monroe,
how long will they go on invoking
your name,
and smearing your legs with oil
in horrible
under-the-counter
magazines,
and certain perverse-benign
gentlemen,
still standing aghast at the sweet
elongation of your breasts,
yellow, pale.

Marilyn, I
only want for them to let you sleep,
lost among the wrong
phone numbers,
or stretched out in the prisons
of your memory:
blonde, feline, and beautiful.

Marilyn, name of faces and charms, swaying
as I call to you,
I only want to see you take your ease
in the empty rooms,
with no hangman, no territories shot with light.
There you are, Marilyn, lying there
like a newly unborn child.

There you are,
my Marilyn, with reddish strands amid the darkness
and a smile
that, finally, is real,
that doesn't lie
when it cries

## Marilyn Monroe

Marilyn Monroe,
hasta cuándo invocan
tu nombre,
y aceitan tus piernas
en horripilantes revistas
de trastiendas,
y algunos perversos-benignos
señores,
contemplan pasmados la dulce
elongación de tus senos,
amarillos, pálidos.

Marilyn, yo
sólo quiero que te dejen dormir,
perdida entre los números equivocados
del teléfono,
o recostada en las cárceles
de tu memoria:
rubia, felina y bella.

Marilyn, nombre de rostros y encantos meciéndose
al llamarte,
yo sólo sé que estás descansando
en los cuartos vacíos,
sin verdugos ni territorios encandilados.
Ahí estás tú, Marilyn, recostada,
como un niño aún recién no nacido.

Ahí estás,
mi Marilyn, con hilos rojizos entre la oscuridad
y una sonrisa
que por fin, es verdadera,
que no miente
cuando llora,
porque quiere el suicidio

from longing for the suicide
of smooth-grained woods
to lay to rest the ravished pubis
the legs the camera caught
among the phosphorescent incantations
of the idle.

How pretty you look, Marilyn Monroe!
beyond all reason, kneeling
with your hands like birds
or stories, coming out
of nightmares,
coming into
light.

de maderas suaves,
para apoyar el pubis ultrajado,
las piernas fotografiadas
entre las fosforescentes encantaciones
de los ociosos.

¡Qué linda te ves Marilyn Monroe!
descabellada hincada,
con tus manos como pájaros
o historias, saliendo
de las pesadillas,
llegando a
la luz.

## Verona

*to Juan*

We plunged desires down
into the house of Juliet
which grew
to believe
through
successive jolts of fire.

In the house of Juliet
after dawn had broken
we wrote some
names and repetitions
that glow on down the lengths of time.

Then,
we tied our
hands
telling lies in the falseness
of the night,
in that place
that still did not exist.

## Verona

*A Juan*

Hundíamos deseos
en casa de Julieta
que llegó a ser
crédula
gracias a la
intermitencia del fuego.

En casa de Julieta
más tarde que el alba,
escribimos algunos
nombres y repeticiones
que brillan tras la longitud del tiempo.

Entonces,
nos amarramos las
manos
mintiendo en las falsedades
de la noche,
en ese lugar
que aún, no existía.

## Country Zones

A hand
strokes down
my back,
as in a scene out of
wild
yellow zones.

That hand
centers on
my silences,
finds the weakness
of my skirt,
comes back round
to the beginning of
my palms,
and I
take pleasure in it
and I
bite it
in the
zone of
silence.

## Zonas de campo

Una mano
acaricia
mi espalda,
como en una escena
de intempestuosas
zonas amarillas.

Esa mano,
se centra en
mis silencios,
encuentra la
debilidad
de mi falda,
regresa
al comienzo de
mis palmas,
y yo,
la gozo,
y yo
la muerdo
en la
zona del
silencio.

## Tulum

They gathered sacred
stones,
and with the natural
light
of air and
memory,
they traced
the characters
of time,
inscribed
their names
in the mirror
of the
sea.

## Tulum

Recogían piedrecillas
sagradas,
y con la luz
natural
del aire y
la memoria,
dibujaban
las letras
del tiempo
inscribían
sus nombres
en el espejo
del
mar.

## Letters

A long-ago surprise, a few dead fireflies,
slither through the letters massed of water, through
the leaves of life
How to tell you of letters and goodbyes
in a drop of absence?
How to speak to you, my love, of the territory
of the fire in a
word?
How to fill you full of shimmerings, of bubblings
of silence and
times spent waiting
of this letter
how it is perfumed
is drunk in, opened,
till it comes
to the chalice of your hands
that look at me
across the sea
of ink
now sailed.

## Cartas

Un antiguo asombro, unas luciérnagas muertas,
se escurren entre las cartas de agua, entre
las hojas de la vida.
¿Cómo contarte de cartas y adioses dentro
de una gota de ausencia?
¿Cómo hablarte dulce mío del territorio
del fuego en una
palabra?
Y cómo llenarte de brillos, de burbujas
de silencio y
esperas,
de esta carta,
que se perfuma,
se bebe, se destapa,
hasta llegar
al cáliz
de tus manos
que me miran
por el mar
de la tinta
navegada.

## Letters in the Fire

You burned my letters with a certain pleasure
with the fearful
haste of
cowards,
because they harbored
fingers, toes, and nails,
processions
of what could never be,
caresses strung across
two burnt-out
constellations.

You burnt the
letters
of this witch
who naked
without daggers
stirred up
the dreary
scenes
of, just possibly,
the truth.

## Cartas en las hogueras

Quemabas con leve placer mis cartas
en la pavorosa
prisa de
los miedosos,
porque en ellas,
había dedos, uñas,
cortejos, de lo
que no pudo ser,
caricias tendidas
en dos agotadas
constelaciones.

Quemabas las
cartas
de esta bruja
que desnuda
y sin puñales
revolvía
las fúnebres
escenas
de una posible
verdad.

## Halves

*Bolivia*

You preferred to make
love
in among the shoes,
to pull discreet doors shut,
and with your worst-dressed
tie
caress me
in the half light.

You were so
afraid
that you only
managed pleasure in
half of
distant
sex.
Half in
light,
half in
night,
in half
a single
bed.

Never touching bottom,
we never got
beyond
the smells of no one
that lingered in the bedrooms
of a hotel here and gone
in
half
a city.

## Mitades

*Bolivia*

Preferías hacer
el amor
entre los
zapatos,
cerrar las puertas discretas,
y con tu mal vestida
corbata
acariciarme
a media luz.

Tanto miedo
tenías
que sólo
gozabas
de la mitad del
sexo
distante.
La mitad de
la luz,
la mitad
de la noche,
en una mitad
de cama
sola.

Sin nunca tocar a fondo,
no alcanzamos
más que
los olores a nadie
que quedan en las alcobas
de un hotel pasajero
en la
mitad
de una ciudad.

## Winter on the Beaches

*to Juan*

You come, alarmed and naked
with the mouths left queasy
by the twists and turns of the rivers of the tides
we are a beach in haughty winter
we are a rocky stretch
unearthed by
seaside scenes.

The angry winter wind
lashes at us.
We remain remote, beyond
the footprints trailing out
from wary sands.

Someone wanders lost among the
lost shoes, sandy
from green depths.

You beat against me lightly
on this hellish winter beach
a mass of flowers and black moss sea gulls
I am a hunching tide
of tangles, lost like
those shoes, or a pail abandoned
by some
sick
child.

## Invierno de las playas

*A Juan*

Llegas, sobresaltado y desnudo
con las bocas mareadas,
trastornadas por los ríos de las mareas,
somos, una playa en el invierno arrogante,
somos, una extensión de roqueríos
desenterrados por las
escenas de la playa.

Nos azota el iracundo viento del
invierno estridente.
Remotos, más lejanos
que las huellas desplegadas
desde las arenas sigilosas somos.

Alguien se extravía entre los
zapatos perdidos arenosos de
muertes verdes.

Tú, me golpeas suavemente
en esta playa infernal del invierno
plasmada de flores y gaviotas de musgos negros.
Yo soy una marea encorvada
de madejas, extraviada como esos
zapatos, o un balde abandonado
por un
niño enfermo.

## Maps

*to Rodrigo Díaz*

I've never read
maps
navigators' charts
because true navigations
are nothing more than
                                        two or three lines
in the palm of the hand
or a random flash
of open sky.

I chose, with wisdom
and disdain, to wander off
among the crusts of bark
or the burning hearthwood.

I wanted the impossible
permanence of
stones
or a summertime of indecipherable
plush moss.

I favored the unheeded
lands,
oceanic inventions
of dispossessed bottles
from which I could
return
gasping but
unconquered
to the definitive
guidelines
of your
hands.

## Mapas

*A Rodrigo Díaz*

Nunca he leído
mapas ni
cartas náuticas,
porque las verdaderas navegaciones
no son más que
dos o tres líneas
de mano
o un azar de cielo
abierto.

Elegí con sabiduría
y desdén, perderme
entre las cortezas
o la leña que arde.

Quise la imposible
permanencia de las
piedras
o un verano de indescifrables
musgos tupidos.

Preferí los territorios
jamás señalados,
las oceánicas invenciones
de botellas desposeídas,
para así,
regresar
jadeante pero
no vencida
a la definitiva
dirección
de tus
manos.

## The Mouths of Hair

She wasn't asking him
to swear
eternal love.
Or for a house,
a bed,
or for oblivion.

Only for illusions.
To get to see him,
think him,
recreate him,
tell him,
imagine him,
dream him,
say him,
celebrate his
hair.

## Las bocas del cabello

No buscaba
los juramentos
del amor eterno.
Ni casa,
cama
u olvido.

Sólo ilusiones.
Poder verlo,
pensarlo,
recrearlo,
contarlo,
imaginarlo,
soñarlo,
decirlo,
celebrar sus
cabellos.

# *Urdimbres entre las hogueras*

---

# *Webs Spun Among the Fires*

## Landscapes from Out of the Mist

Autumn, autumnal, defenseless witness, soaking in the moss,
leaves
folded to the breathing of the season. We wonder whether
to breathe in the devilish delight of the leaves enfolding us
tighter and tighter down by the mists. We wonder whether to be
winds or bees displaced in the cadences of this perverse mist.

Look at that misbegotten shadow lurking after us, spying on us
from
behind the dusty panes. In this autumn time of no return, of no
alternative
I ask you to bite into me, like an apple tree spread out across
warm fields so you'll come upon me and my
neck, strangled like a crackling leaf, a crackling
strangled thing.

## Paisajes de entre la niebla

Otoño, otoñales, indefenso testigo, absorbe musgos, hojas
plegadas al aliento de la estación. Dudamos
si respirar la delicia diabólica de las hojas que nos estrechan
más y más junto a las nieblas. Dudamos si ser vientos o
abejas trastocadas en las cadencias de esta niebla perversa.

Mira esa sombra malograda acechándonos, espiándonos tras
cristales empolvados. En este otoño sin regresos ni alternativas,
te pido que me muerdas, como un manzano derramándose por los
prados caídos para que así tropieces conmigo y con mi
cuello que se ahorca como una hoja crepitando, crepitante
ahorcada.

## Meditation on Hands

Time and time again we've tried just holding
hands to see the favorable return of well-wishing bats,
or simply fire, wine, blankets, your hands on
my skirt, which opens and falls back when you name me and there
I am.

What we love are the flour hands of a
child like dreams of what we could be.

Reach out to me, come to me, bite into me, feel me, know me like a
yellow wave
conquer me, cover me, moist and wordless like the
silent waves along benign shores.

Pierce me through
like the open hand
like a dome, a goblet or a word
translated in a figure
rising up and
creeping over eyelids,
perching like a languid butterfly
in the yellow
of eyes held shut
and like a pirate
opening treasure troves
of nightmare
with a quiet
restful hand.

Love me with those old hands, tired of taking notes on life
of setting poems down into the thick black handwriting of vanity,
of a
poem misread as sonorous.

## Meditación sobre las manos

Hemos intentado una y otra vez más simplemente tomarnos de la
mano para ver el favorable regreso de benignos murciélagos
o simplemente el fuego, el vino, las mantas, las manos tuyas
sobre
mi falda que se abre y se repliega cuando me nombras y estoy.

Lo que queremos son las manos de harina de un
niño como los sueños de lo que pudimos ser.

Dame la mano, llégame, muérdeme, siénteme, séme como una ola
amarilla
vénceme, cúbreme, humedecida y muda como las
silenciosas olas de benignas orillas.

Atraviésame,
como la mano abierta
como cúpula, copa o palabra
traducida en una figura
que se alza y
trepa por los párpados, se
posa como una mariposa lánguida
entre el amarillo
de los ojos cerrados
y como un pirata
destapa los tesoros
de la pesadilla
con una mano reposada
quieta.

Quiéreme con esas manos viejas, cansadas de anotar la vida,
de escribir poemas con la pesada letra negra de la vanidad, de un
poeta incomprendidamente sonoro.

Come,
I am here
to pardon sorrows,
to be a lighthouse like the gentle, luminous Chilean peaches
come, without the fog of those who never learned how to forget,
hold me down, tie my bonds
dance me,
touch me with your hands
with your fingertips
read me in the moist prophetic blindness
of hands that
know themselves to be
your own.

Ven
yo estoy aquí
para perdonar tristezas,
para ser un faro como los suaves y luminosos duraznos chilenos.
Ven, sin la bruma de los que no saben olvidar, sujétame,
amárrame

báilame
tócame con las manos
con las yemas,
léeme en la ceguedad húmeda y profética
de las manos que se saben
tuyas.

## Remembering

Remembering wasn't dangerous,
because in silence
she could be an
open vault,
a jungle harmless
to invent.
And she remembered light slicing through his naked body against
a blue swatch of time.
She remembered the words his mouth, like smoke, traced out,
down the walkways and murmurs, across the city with no sea.

How she liked remembering
the monotonous stroll along
the beach
or the sandy shadows
following her tracks.
She recalled the shifting
pathways of the tides
and, in those hours, pronounced
the movement of the waves
kisses up against the rocks
everything, just to keep remembering: calling-loving-writing.

In her great long journals, in between her fingers,
she memorized those ordinary
names,
those mild-mannered passers-by
who disappeared
but not from her memory,
because she called out, screamed, and her thin hands wrote
the message of papyrus scrolls
into the blue bottles
that sailed off, not just drifting on the sea.

# Recordar

Recordar no era peligroso,
porque en el silencio
ella podía ser una
bóveda abierta,
una selva benigna para
inventar.
Y ella recordaba la luz atravesando su cuerpo desnudo frente a un trozo
azul de tiempo.
Recordaba las palabras que su boca, como el humo, iban trazando
en los paseos y murmuros por una ciudad sin mar.

Cuánto le gustaba recordar,
la monótona travesía por
la playa
o las sombras de arena que
seguían sus huellas.
Ella, recordaba el rumbo
incierto de las mareas
y entre las horas, pronunciaba
el movimiento de las olas,
los besos contra el roquerío
todo, para poder recordar: llamar-amar-escribir.

En sus inmensos cuadernos, entre sus dedos,
ella memorizaba aquellos nombres de
todos los días,
aquellos mansos transeúntes
que desaparecieron
pero no de su recuerdo,
porque ella, llamaba, gritaba y sus delgadas manos escribían
el mensaje de los papiros,
en las botellas azules
que navegaban no a una deriva.

She remembered her
travels
across the ancient skin
of the one who abandoned her driven by oblivion
and she thought him back,
sending him gold filaments that peeled off from the roundness
of a dream
dreamed so often
just to name him
by dreaming him
just to dream him
by naming him.

Ella recordaba sus
viajes
por la piel antigua
del que la abandonó por la manía del olvido,
y ella, lo pensaba,
mandándole hebras doradas que se desprendían de la redondez
de un sueño,
soñado tantas veces
sólo para nombrarlo
soñándolo
sólo para
soñarlo
nombrándolo.

## Day

Day, like a spread of winds with no fear
of shaven memory. Hatred stretches out
between us like a haughty amputee.

This day is the crystal of a whip or feverish parts. Everything
explodes and runs across my roughened forehead, everything
explodes above the
smoke, the plazas, the scenes of conquered lands. Although
today, it's no good understanding, since she's combing out her hair
half a century and more on the corner edge of fear.

And suddenly, the afternoon swears to be inflamed,
phosphorescent. It's
ushered in among the markings of the bones. The shadow now
weighs
in, my waist becomes a witches' sabbath dancing on its own. You,
impossible, come down like an exhausted Lazarus, striking the
defeated bodies of the living. Dead, impenetrable, you, so
alien among a dead king's thistlethorns, you play at burning me
in the bonfires beating at my faces and my lands.

## El día

El día, como un mantel de vientos que no teme a
la memoria rapada. El odio se extiende
entre nosotros como un soberano manco.

Este día, es el cristal de un látigo o piezas afiebradas. Todo
estalla y recorre mi frente áspera, todo estalla sobre los
humos, las plazas, las escenas de países vencidos. Aunque en
este día, nada se saca con comprender porque ella se peina
hace más de medio siglo en las esquinas del miedo.

Y de pronto, la tarde se jura iracunda, fosforescente. Se
anuncia entre los indicios de los huesos. Llega el peso de la
sombra, mi cintura es un aquelarre bailándose solitaria. Tú,
imposible, desciendes como un Lázaro agotado, atropellando los
vencidos cuerpos de los vivos. Muerto, impenetrable, tú, tan
ajeno entre las espinas de un rey muerto, tú, juegas a quemarte
en las hogueras que golpean mis rostros y mis paisajes.

# Night

All night long, the restless rain attacking, full of pain, like
oblivion or the wounds of love, oozing crimson drops
beyond the thresholds of desirable prisons. All night long shining
on me,
enveloping my low-life bones. Mute, night is
voice to the ceremony that responds in garbled disarray; it's
silence
seeking you out like a murderer's hand.

Rain, Rodrigo Díaz, like a call horn of black
sirens summons you, hides you out behind perverted mouthfuls of
a solitary pillow lost out in the sirens' sea.
Rain awakens your transparent body, makes its way across
your clammy body, clammy like the moss that only
flowers in the flush of sex, of love and fear.

I want never to go back to the empty room with its plaster
ceiling. It rains so much.
A figure of the made-up woods, I want only to be Juliet,
to set your face afire, to offer you a drink of water, the
roundness of
oranges, tides, wine-drinking nights,
bodies sheltering in the arms of the malicious rain.

Rain comes down, we lie subdued between your shadow and my
own. You are an arm embracing me, a word that ages me, a smile
of moistened thighs.

Naked, bodies multiply like
rain in a sheath of rivers. Darkness is not reckless
rain runs across our faces, and you and I embrace
to make our way across a waterscape.

## La noche

Toda la noche, la lluvia inquieta embestida, dolorida como el
olvido o las heridas del amor, que despiden unas gotas carmesíes
tras los umbrales de calabozos deseables. Toda la noche
brillándome,
envolviéndome los huesos de la mala muerte. Muda la noche es
la voz de la ceremonia que replica trastornada; es el silencio
que te busca como una mano asesina.

La lluvia Rodrigo Díaz como una bocina de sirenas
negras te llama, te oculta tras las perversas bocanadas de
una almohada solitaria perdida en el mar de las sirenas.
La lluvia despierta, tu cuerpo transparente, desfila por
tu cuerpo muy frío, muy frío, como el musgo que sólo
florece en los arreboles del sexo, del amor y del espanto.

Yo no quiero regresar al cuarto vacío del cielo raso. Llueve
mucho
muñeco de los bosques inventados, yo sólo quiero ser Julieta
para encender tu rostro, ofrecerte el agua, la redondez de las
naranjas, las mareas, las noches para beber vino, los
cuerpos que se cobijan bajo el abrazo de la lluvia maliciosa.

Llueve, estamos quietos entre tu sombra y la mía. Tú eres un
brazo que me abraza, una palabra que me envejece, una sonrisa
de muslos humedecidos.

Desnudos los cuerpos se multiplican como
la lluvia en su túnica de ríos. La oscuridad no es temeraria,
la lluvia cruza nuestros rostros, y tú y yo, nos abrazamos
para cruzar una pintura de aguas.

## Undoing Braids

After the wintered mirrors,
and always in the fires,
I Marjorie Agosín
let my hair fall free
taken in your fingers, it's a wellspring
of crimes cradled
in the delicious ebb tide
of forbidden drifting.

I am a vain woman
in love with spaces and their afterburns.
In them I carry on the silence
of enchantment,
the struggles waged by my dead sisters
with their long high hair, standing out among the
crypts.

You brush it out,
it grows so thickly in your hands,
two wings amassed of space and time.

Look how my hair opens wide
like peering
from the inconclusive threshold of some door
and she sees but stays unseen, flowering, memoryless,
full of hair on that other threshold.

Our mingled hair
lies upon the nightfallen
islands of desire,
burns us deep,

like steep, narrow fields of sugar cane
it feels you out, draping crumpled, limp

## Destapándose las trenzas

Después de los invernados espejos,
y siempre en las hogueras,
yo Marjorie Agosín,
me desato los cabellos
que entre tus yemas, son un manantial
de crímenes meciéndose
en la deliciosa resaca
de una deriva prohibida.

Soy una vanidosa,
una enamorada de sus espacios y de sus rescoldos.
En ellos, llevo el silencio
de los hechizos,
el litigio de mis hermanas muertas,
de larguísimos cabellos altos, sobresaliendo entre las criptas.

Tú, los cepillas,
crecen tan espesos junto a tus manos,
son dos alas consteladas de espacios y tiempos.

Mira como se abren mis cabellos
como quien se asoma
en el umbral inconcluso de alguna puerta,
y ella se va sin ser vista, florecida, desmemoriada
llena de cabellos en ese otro umbral.

Los cabellos nuestros
reposan en las islas
anochecidas del deseo,
nos queman mucho,

al igual que cañaverales hondos y angostos
te palpan, y se extienden desmoronados

across your neck,
bleeding out in loves.

My hair and yours
are like rivers
singing down your
back, with its
coves and bays.

With dawn awakening
my hair takes on a fresh, sure form
where you lay in sleep.
It becomes the edges of red roses, red slippers
fires with no shadow
fires you cradle in your palms
fires in the violent invention of your hands.

por tu nuca
desangrándose en quereres.

Mis cabellos, en los tuyos
son como los ríos
que cantan sobre tus
espaldas pobladas de
grutas y bahías.

Amanece, amaneciendo
mis cabellos se estilan frescos seguros
después de tu sueño sobre ellos.
Y son, orillas de rosas rojas, zapatillas rojas
hogueras sin sombra
hogueras entre tus palmas
hogueras en la violenta invención de tus manos.

## Miniature Voyage

*The body remembers a love,*
*like lighting the lamp*
Alejandra Pizarnik

In a woods, we passed through night, alone, all alone,
adrift. We gathered scraps of forest, sundown incantations.
Alone, all alone in the vagueness of returning to a house set on
edge
by the fire of silence, like a swarming, restless promise.

Alone at the edge of thresholds, spare and plain, just the
roundness
of fire on our mouths. We began undressing to slough off
the trappings of hatred, and you still have branches left across
your face and
your arms still bring back to me the smell of poisons.

Naked, in a Spanish shawl, alone, we are no longer, though the
death
of the culprits and of those who love, hiding in the noises of the
old house, comes creeping round here, rapt and spellbound.

We are like a field of poppies, a single row of tulips. Suns
and moons seep through our eyes and our bodies
settle in for love, and the body dreams to remember love.

Alone, all alone, but less alone now, imagining ourselves on a
miniature
voyage from your mouth to mine.

## Diminuta travesía

*El cuerpo se acuerda de un amor,*
*como encender la lámpara.*
Alejandra Pizarnik

En un bosque, cruzamos la noche, solos, solísimos,
y a la deriva. Recogimos pedazos de florestas encantaciones del
atardecer.
Solos, solísimos en la vaguedad de los regresos a una casa erizada
por el fuego del silencio, como una promesa pululante e
inquieta.

Solos al borde de los umbrales, sin lujos ni atuendos, sólo
la redondez
del fuego sobre nuestras bocas. Comenzamos a desnudarnos,
despojarnos
de los atuendos del odio, y aún te quedan ramas en tu rostro
y aún
tus brazos me recuerdan el olor de los venenos.

Desnudos, en una manta castellana, solos, ya no estamos, aunque
la muerte
de los culpables y los que se aman escondiéndose en el rumor
de la
casa vieja, ronda absorta y encantada.

Parecemos un campo de amapolas, una sola franja de tulipanes.
Se
filtran los soles y las lunas entre nuestros ojos y los cuerpos
se acomodan para el amor, y el cuerpo sueña para acordarse del
amor.

Solos tan solos, pero ahora menos solos, imaginándonos en una
diminuta
travesía desde tu boca a la mía.